Cars and Trucks and Things

in Signed English

Text: HOWARD L. ROY

Illustrations: RALPH R. MILLER, Sr.

Prepared under the supervision of the staff
of the Gallaudet Signed English Project:

HARRY BORNSTEIN, Director
KAREN LUCZAK SAULNIER
LILLIAN B. HAMILTON

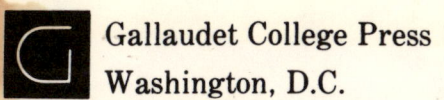

Gallaudet College Press
Washington, D.C.

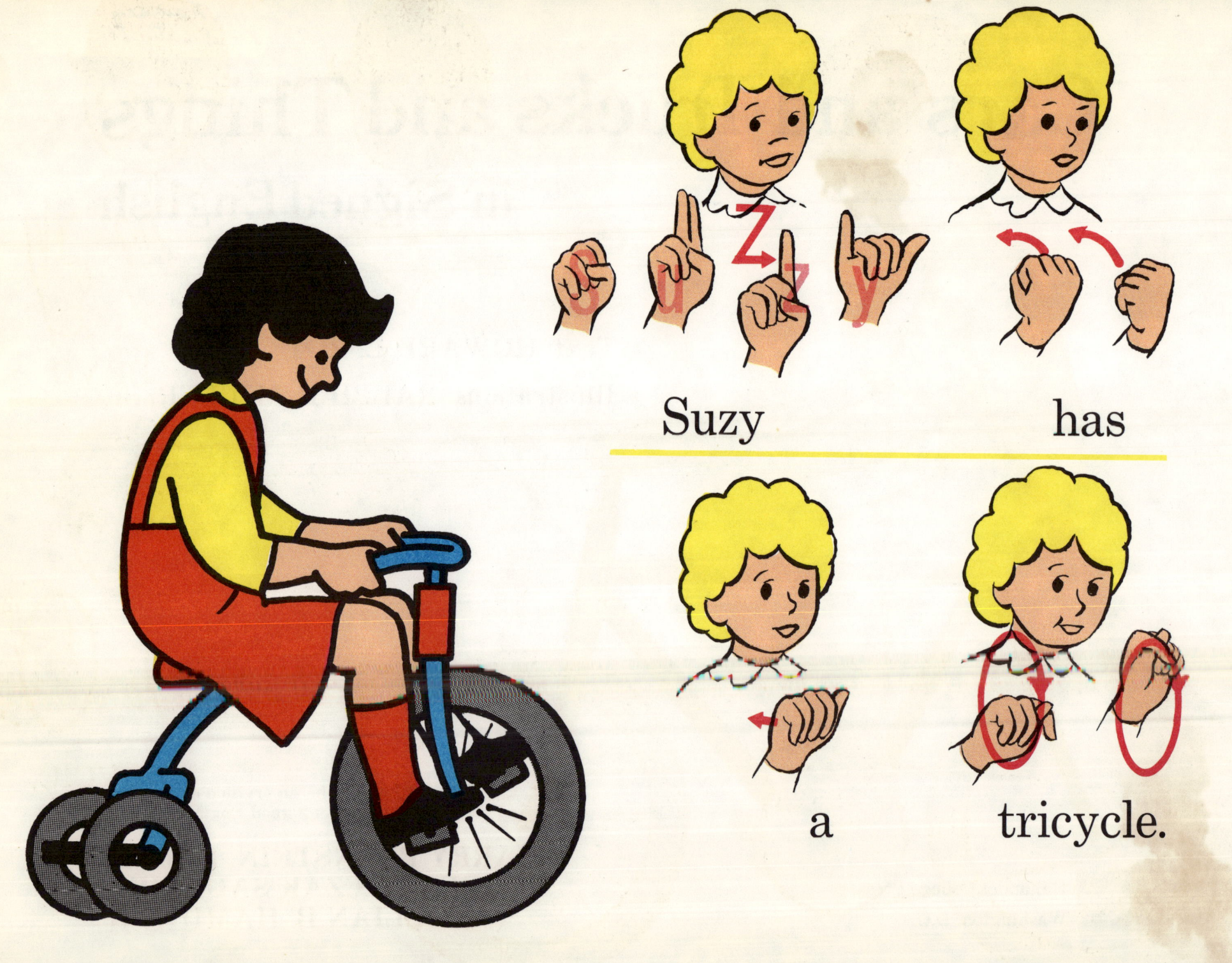

We have a new car.

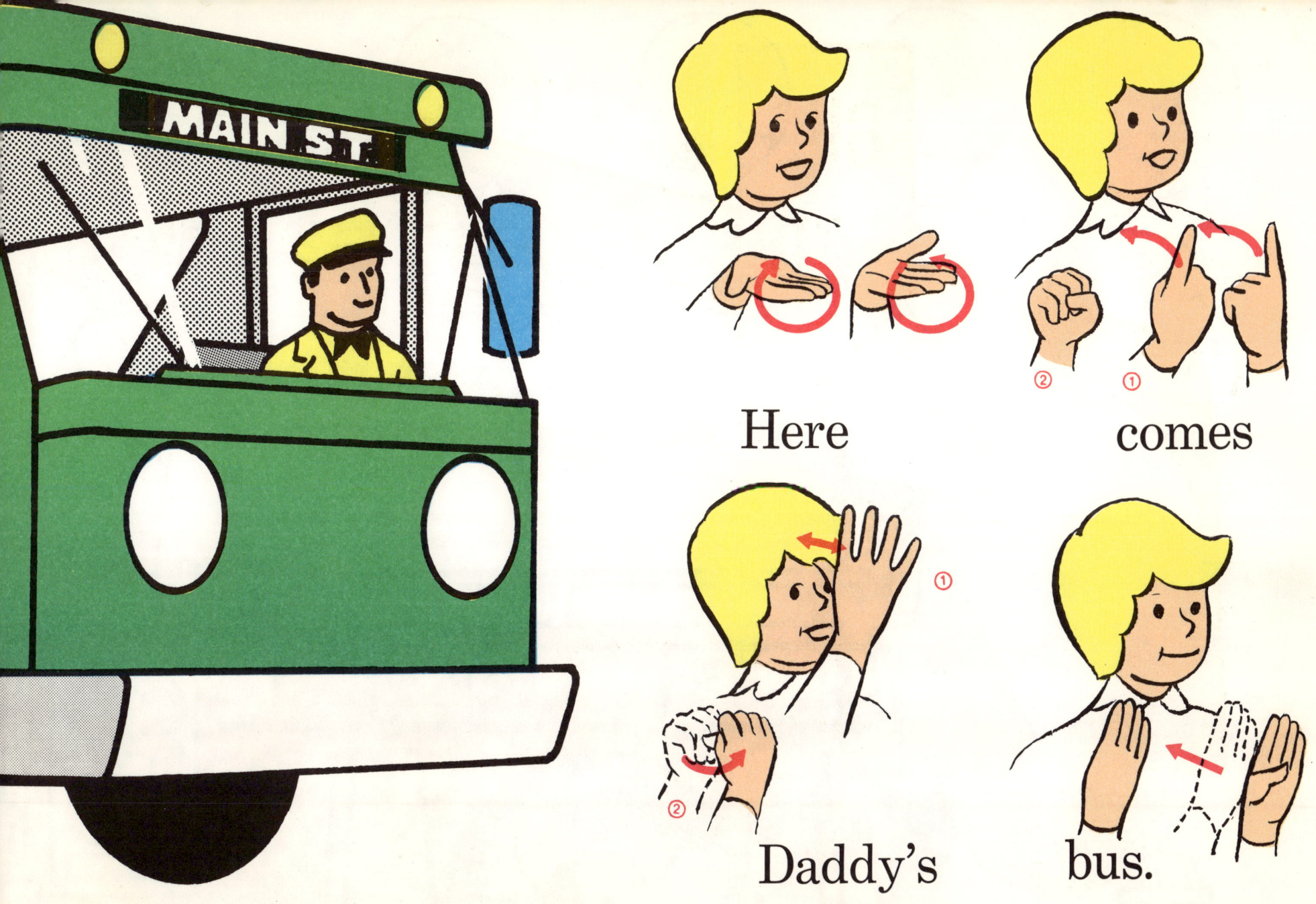

When I am big, I'll

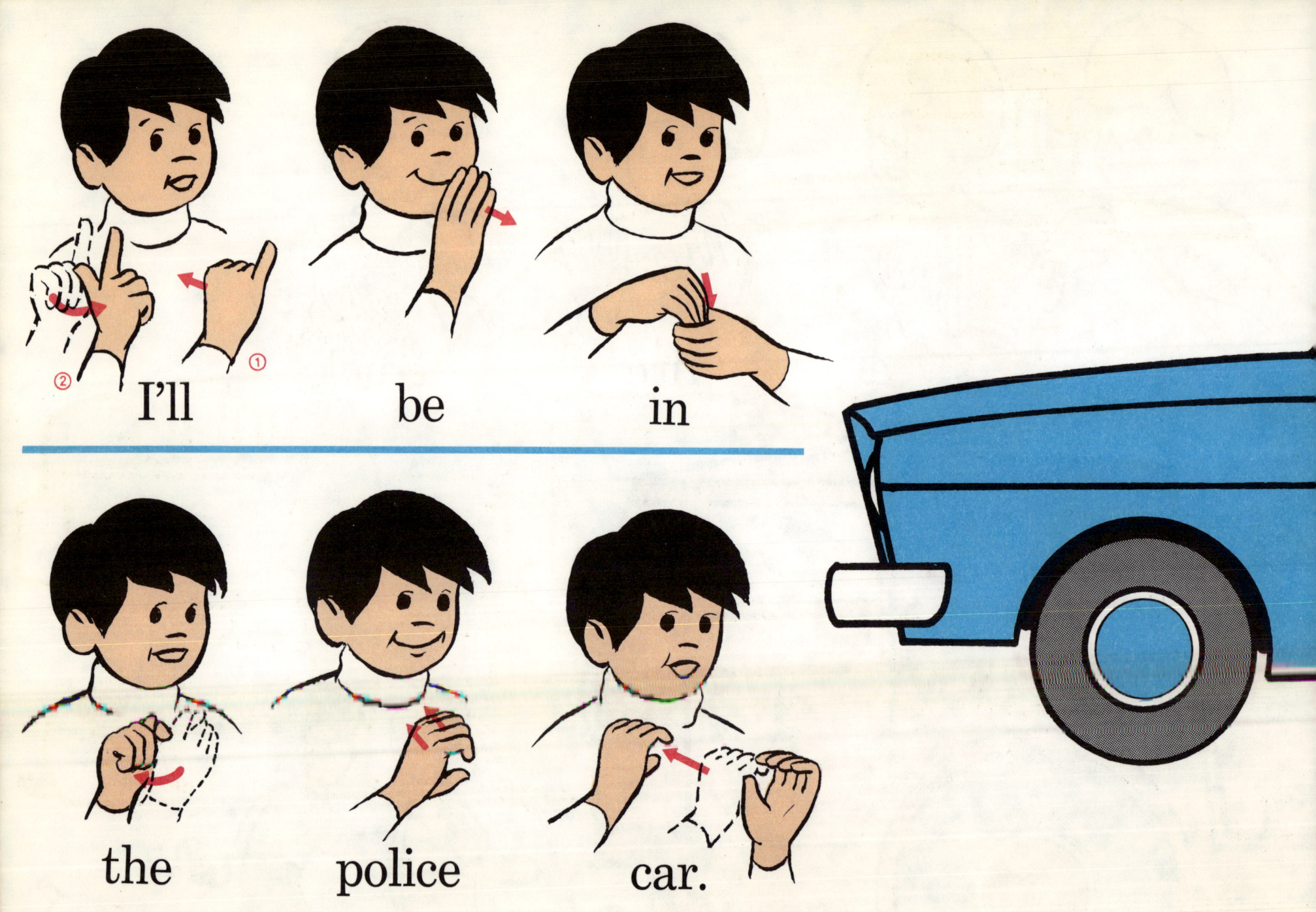

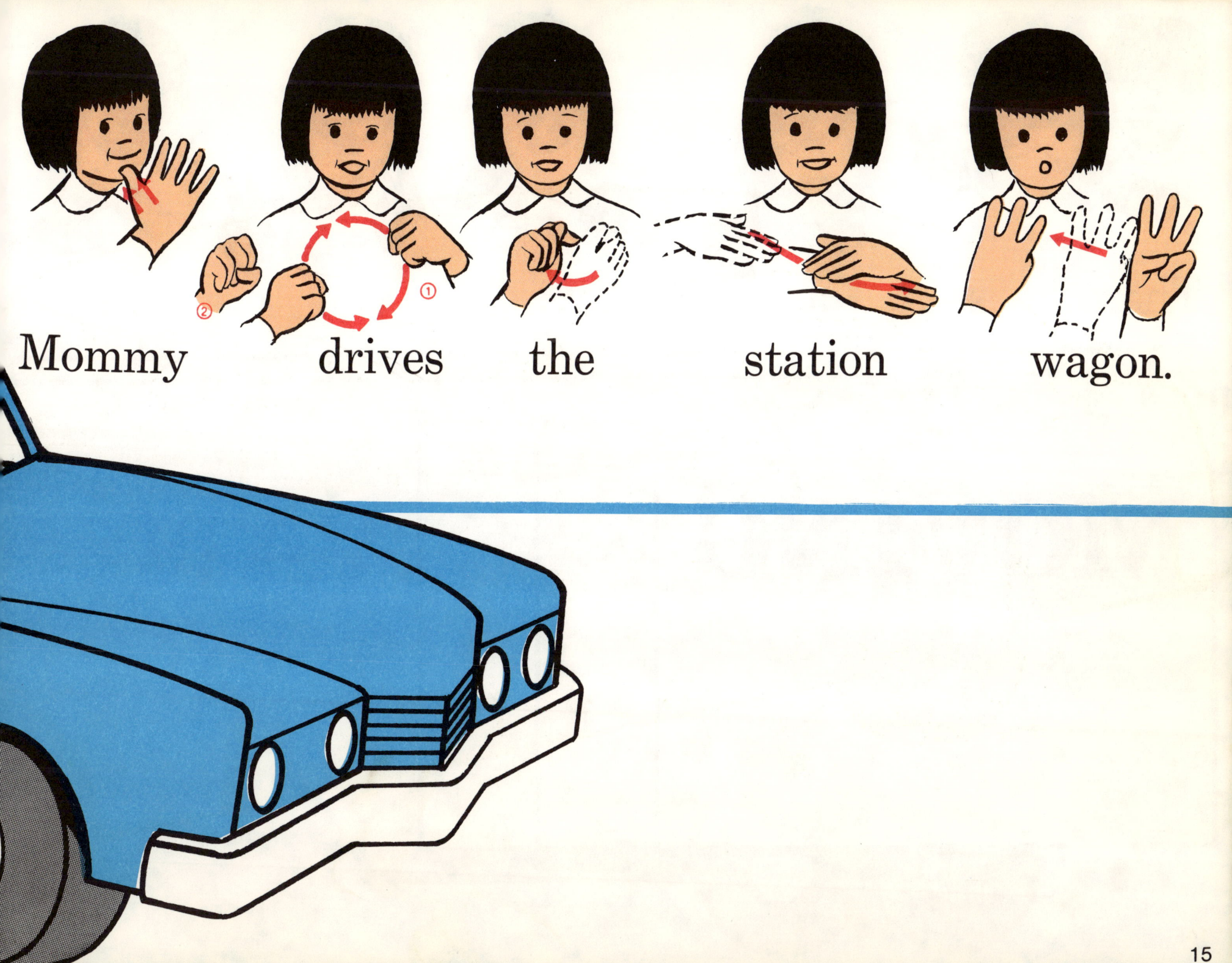

There is a moving van at

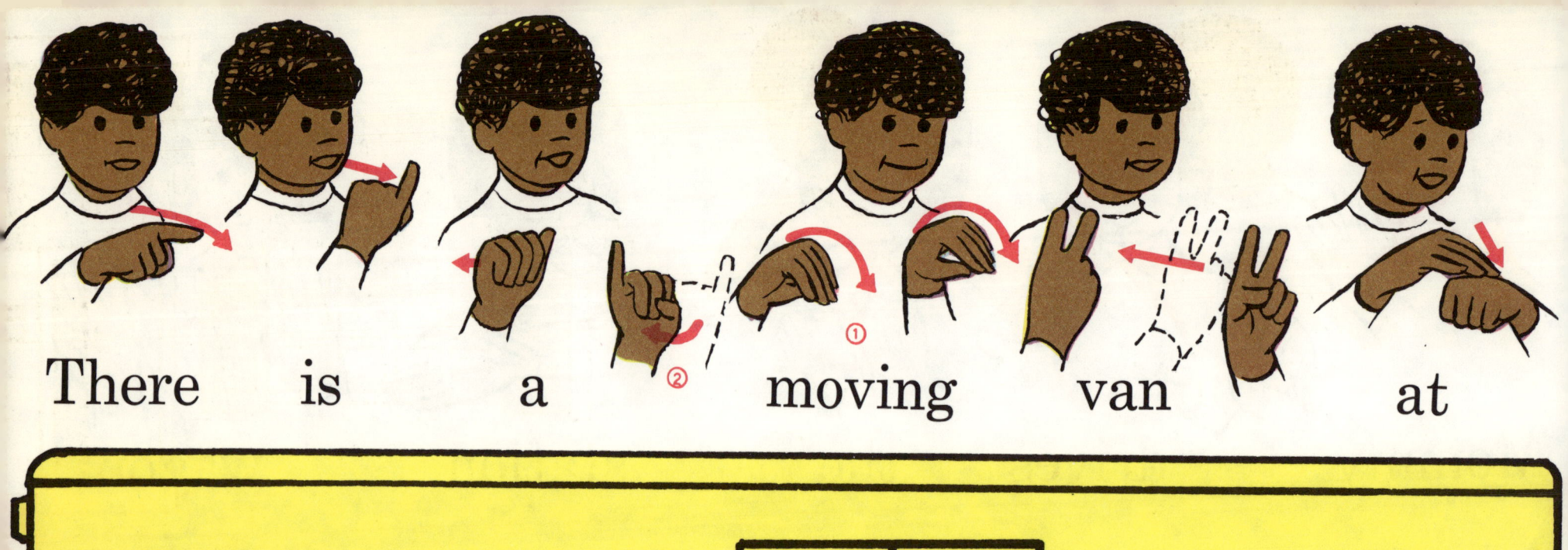

MOVING VAN

The dump truck hauls dirt.

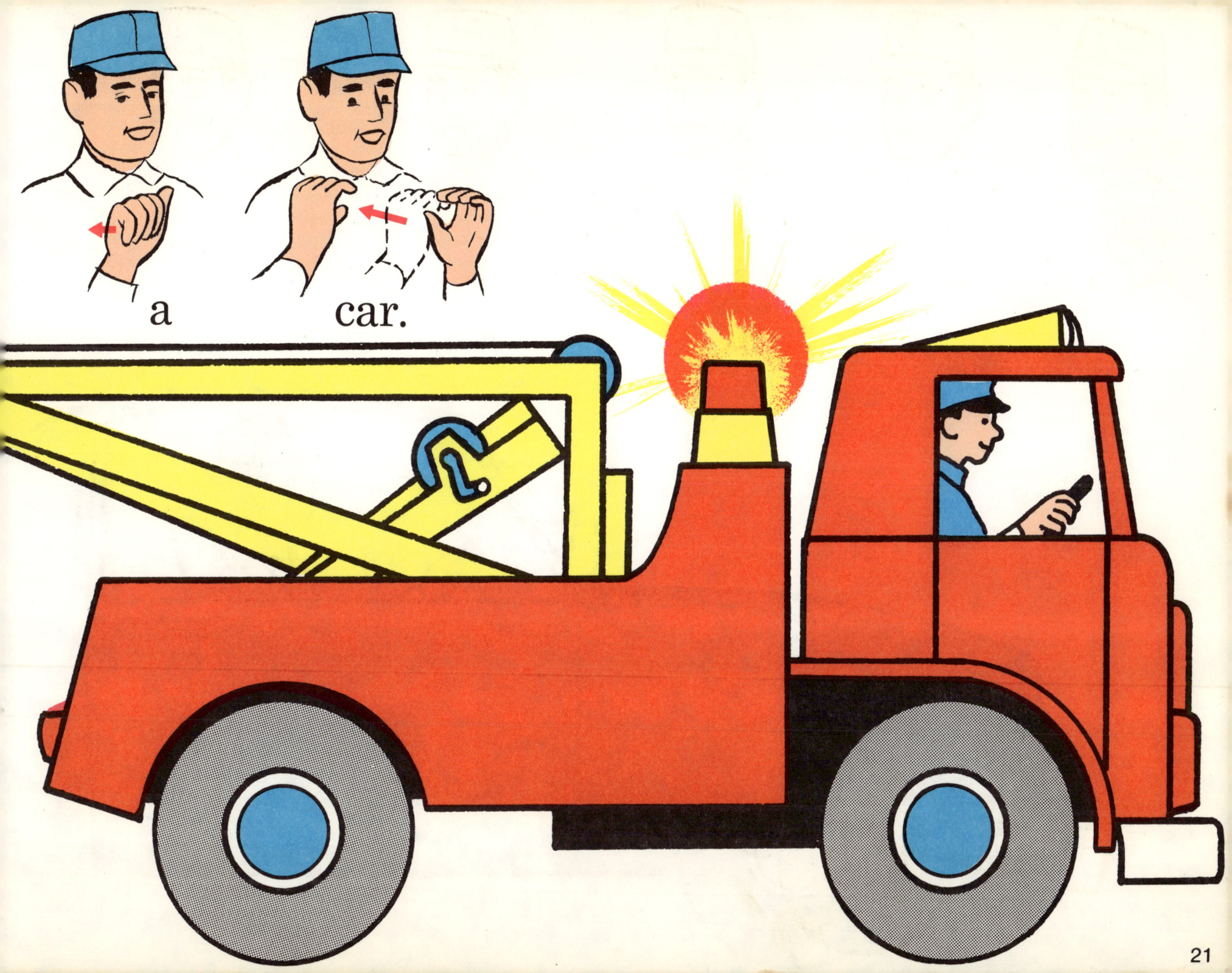

We are going in a taxi.

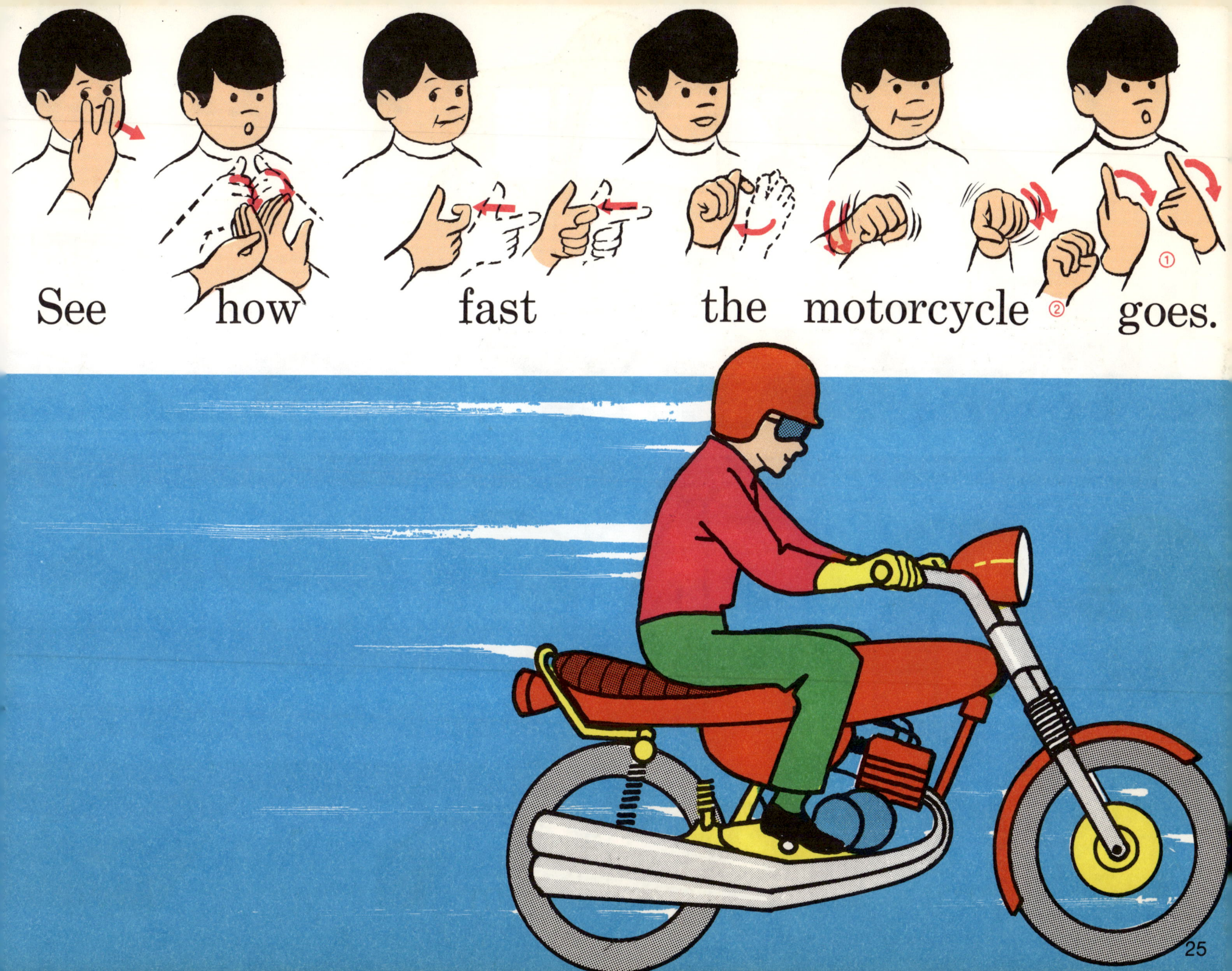

See the jeep going up the hill!

This is a sports car.

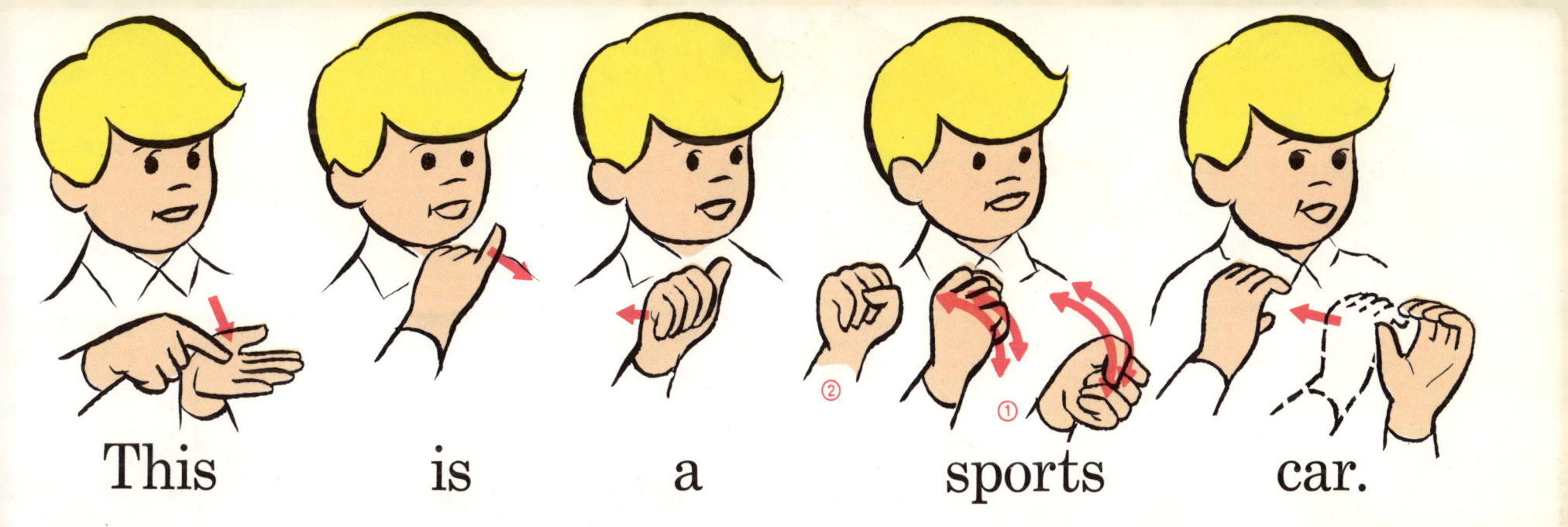

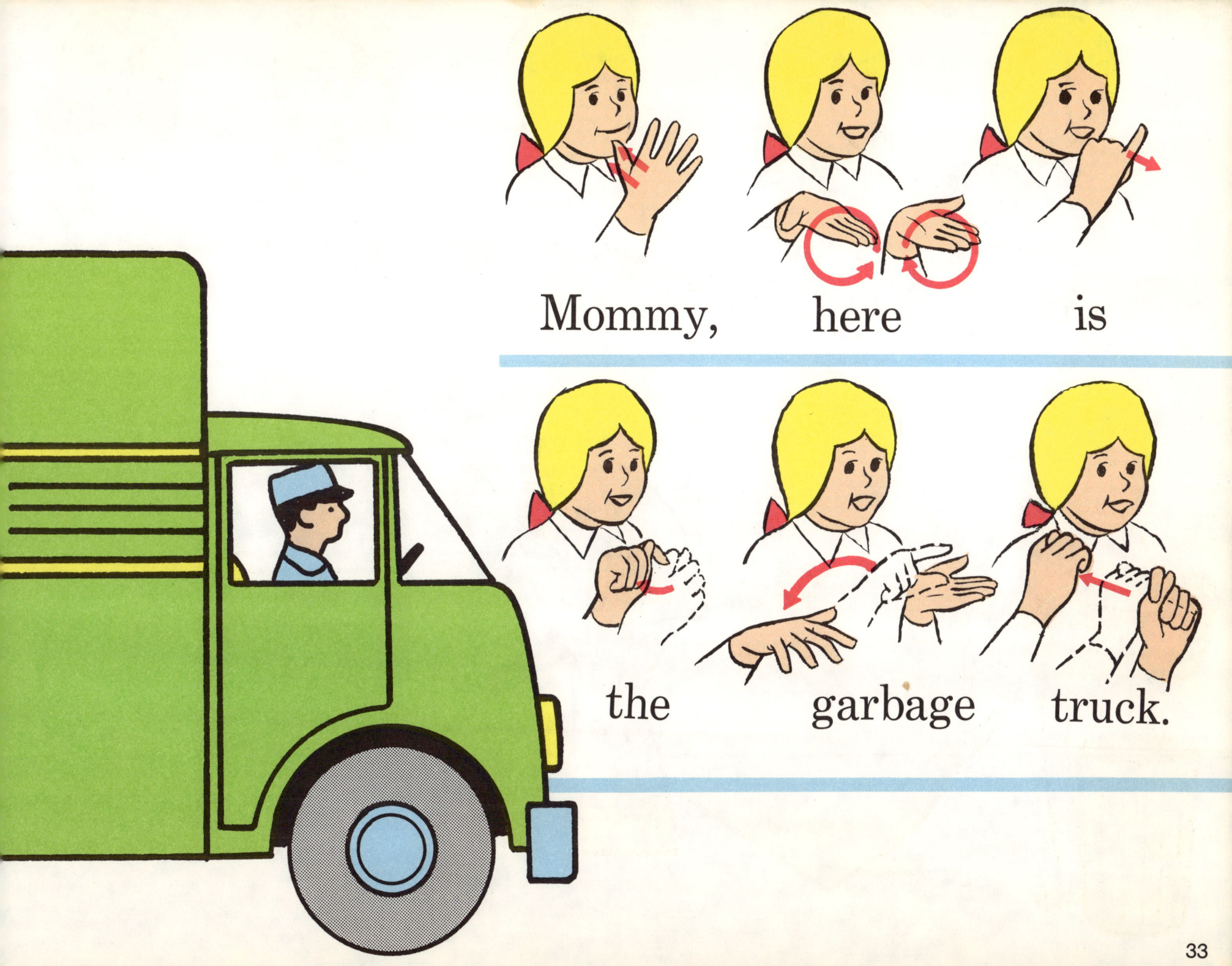

The mail truck picks up

our   mail.

Index*

A	2	Haul	27	Police	12
Are	16	Hauls	18	Picks	34
At	24	Have	3		
		Here	9	Ride	7
Be	12	Hill	30	Rides	5
Bicycle	3	House	17		
Beg	10	How	25	School	5
Bus	5			See	25
		I	2	Sport	7
Car	6	Ice cream	29	Sports	31
Carrier	27	I'll	12	Station	15
Carry	23	I'm	10	Suzy	2
Comes	9	In	5		
		Is	16	Taxi	24
Daddy	9			The	5
Danny's	17	Jeep	30	There	16
Dirt	18	Jennie	5	Things	23
Drives	15			This	31
Dump	18	Let's	7	Tow	20
				Tricycle	2
Every	29	Mail	34	Trailers	23
		Many	23	Truck	18
Fast	25	Morning	15	Trucks	27
		Motorcycle	25		
Garbage	33	Moving	16	Up	30
Give	7				
Going	24	New	5	Van	16
Goes	25				
		Our	35	Wagon	7
Has	2			We	6
				When	10

*First appearance only.